Deep In the Dimension of Pitchforks and Horns

By

Michael Kimball BSN, RN

THE DEVIL AND DR. DUVAL

The Devil and Dr. Duval
sat together and drew a contract
"I'll sell my soul for more alcohol"
said the good doctor as they drew up their pact
and when they finished their bargain
the devil just sat back and laughed
"Our agreement is binding now,
you know you can never go back,
you just signed your soul away
for a lifetime of trouble and grief
and when you die early one day
you'll suffer forever with me.
I'll put you in a corner
where the fire and brimstone are strong
and there you'll pay for all you've done
Deep in the **Dimension of Pitchforks and Horns**

DEEP IN THE DIMENSION OF PITCHFORKS AND HORNS

Deep in the Dimension of Pitchforks and Horns,
there's a scorching hot corner just where I belong
the sky is blood red, there's no sun or moon
the trees are all dead with no leaves in bloom
there's mean rat like creatures and oversized roaches
that crawl up and chomp on whomever approaches
the ground's made of charcoal that incinerates
with heat so intense it can melt off your face
tortuous demons mess with your mind
and you feel schizophrenic as your neurons unwind
disfigured vultures circle and screech
they gnaw on your tongue until you've lost your speech
there's ominous cackling and mischievous snickers
pretty black roses with sharp teeth and whiskers
they tear at your flesh, exposing the bone
I don't wanna be here, I just wanna go home!
But I'm deep in the Dimension of Pitchforks and Horns
Mom, Dad and Greg are gone
I lost my whole family, My Richie, my Dog
I've been so fucking angry for so fucking long
I've forged my own pitchfork, I've earned myself horns
this isn't the dimension where I should belong
so it's time to go back now, it's time to get out
of this place I uncomfortably dwell
I used to think I deserved this place
but no one deserves this hell.

Contents

INTRODUCTION

I wrote this book for you, the addict. I wrote this book for you, the alcoholic. I wrote this book for you, the gambler, the overeater, the sexaholic, the spender, the prisoner of whatever poisonous bars that are holding you back from living your best life. I wrote this book while I was involuntarily committed into an alcohol and substance abuse program, a program that saved my life despite every single odd and intention I had. My name is Michael Kimball and I am dependent on drugs and alcohol, I am a gambler, an overeater, a spender and inherently drawn to whatever poison is available.

I am an addict.

I wrote this book because I didn't know any other way to express how I was feeling and maybe you can relate. Sometimes it is difficult to say what you are feeling, to articulate your emotions. When I am feeling hurt, in pain or vulnerable I tend to express myself in poetry and rhyme. Maybe you can relate to some of this poetry about trauma, loss, sexuality, addiction and recovery. I have a sincere hope that my readers find these entries a source of hope, inspiration and a reminder that despite how we might feel sometimes, we are never alone.

I want to tell you my story but I will try to keep it brief. This will give you some background information into some of the poetry you will read. However, my story is not unique. We all go through dark periods and it is my hope that the poems will speak for themselves, and speak to you.

MY STORY

I struggled with drug use from an early age. At first, I was prescribed narcotics for a tonsillectomy. I immediately loved the feeling, the euphoria, the rush. I loved it so much I pretended to be in agony just to get more of the pain-relieving medicine from my doctor. To my surprise she gave it to me. At some point I realized that my surgical pain was gone and I was strictly using the medicine in order to get high. I didn't care though. The feelings were already too strong. When I ran out of that medicine, I resorted to buying Percocet and Oxycodone off the streets and once I became a nurse, all bets were off. I never took medicine from a patient in pain, ever, but if there was extra or left over narcotics, I found a way to get them into my body.

As one can imagine, my addiction got worse and worse until my life was ruined, my job was terminated and I surrendered my nursing license, rendering me unable to practice any longer. At the time, this was enough to wake me up and get me to stay sober. I quit all narcotics, got another job and began to straighten out my life. It was good for a while, until it wasn't.

For the next decade I did well. I got married, enjoyed married life, started a podcast and was a productive member of my circle and community. I found that I was able to maintain wonderful relationships with friends and family. During this time, I was a social drinker, never considering alcohol another drug that I should be avoiding. That was a mistake. You see, a drug is a drug is a drug. Any substance that alters your body in any way is a drug and that includes alcohol. When life seemed to get too difficult, I found myself relying more and more on alcohol in order to get through the day.

In 2017 my father took ill and needed to be placed on dialysis. Out of his 6 children, I did most of the work to help him in his final years. I did the cooking, cleaning, shopping and transportation to and from doctor's visits. I didn't mind it, I loved it; I was super close to him, and when he passed, it was devastating to me. That's when my drinking went from "social" to habitual. I found myself drinking nips to calm down on the day of his funeral, a stress relief practice I had never done. I didn't realize that this behavior would become an instant and progressive problem, but it did.

As time passed I found myself drinking more and more nips. With Dad gone, I then became the primary caregiver for mom. I did the cooking, cleaning, shopping and transportation to and from doctor's visits. I didn't mind it, I loved it, we grew closer than ever. She became my best friend. I realized, however, that I was starting to neglect myself in small ways. I wouldn't sleep or eat as well as I should. I didn't shower or change my clothing as routinely. I was tired. I was more emotional; sensitive.

On top of taking care of Mom, I found myself also providing care for my husband's grandparents. I did the cooking, some cleaning, shopping and would often accompany them on doctor's visits. I assisted with all health care needs, walks, exercise, property maintenance etc. I didn't mind it, I loved it. I developed a love for them like I never knew, but the self-neglect only grew.

Before I knew it I was splitting my week up so that I could be with mom (who lived nearly two hours away) on the weekends and the grandparents during the week. I managed to do all this and still make sure to take care of my own house and husband, our meals and chores. Basically, for several years all my time was spent caring for everyone else, everyone else, that is….but me.

This pattern of self-neglect took its toll. I began to realize how little those around me were doing to help our loved ones in need. Many family members sat back and watched as I slowly burnt out. Many of mom's relatives lived a very short distance from her, unlike myself, yet despite their constant pledges to "be there for her" they rarely were, at least in the practical sense.

On the other end of things, my in-laws thanked me often for taking care of the grandparents, they often even helped financially as I was not generating an income. Still, they watched me decline over a short period, mentally and physically. They blindly attributed my burn out to mental illness. Not once did anyone ever sit down with me and try to have an honest open conversation about what was going on.

My husband, having been brought up in a world where everything was handed to him on a silver platter, couldn't understand why I denatured. During our relationship I had grown accustomed to his desire to be idle. I loved him so much that I often overlooked his unwillingness to cook, clean, do household chores and contribute. I was content with his company. But as family life grew increasingly difficult, I found myself frustrated with the heavy workload. How could someone who professed their love so deeply allow me to drown so significantly? I found myself becoming a nag. We would get into arguments often because I felt a significant imbalance in our marital contributions. It got so bad that I dubbed him with the moniker "Mister Exister." His only goal in life seemed to be cuddling in bed with the pets and watching TV as he watched me slowly unravel and become a full-blown alcoholic before his very eyes.

I silently built up resentments toward all of these people and many more. I silently increased my alcohol consumption, slowly, surreptitiously. I was often tempted to ask for help but I just couldn't. They all saw how hard I was working and they already didn't seem to care, so what was the use of me asking for their assistance? Additionally, I also liked things to be done very meticulously and felt that my standards wouldn't be met if those less compassionate (or competent) did all the work I was doing.

As I continued to burnt out, I slowly drank more and the more I drank the angrier I got at those around me who were passively, idly witnessing me fall apart. After all I was doing why didn't anyone take the initiative to help me? Couldn't they see that I was struggling? Couldn't they see that I was burning the candle at both ends? Couldn't they see my personality changing before their very eyes? If so, why didn't they care enough to do something? Why weren't they all willing to go to the same lengths I was going to in order to help family…me? The anger and resentment grew. The drinking continued. The drinking increased.

In the beginning of 2022 mom passed away under some pretty awful circumstances. She had fallen and gotten stuck between her bedside table and bed. I helped her up with a bear hug, got her into bed and begged her to go into the hospital. Acknowledging that she was terminal, she chose not to go. She died that night while holding my hand.

When Mom's death certificate came in the mail it noted that her cause of death was a stomach bleed. For the longest time I quietly blamed myself for her death. After all, when I picked her up from her fall I had to put some pressure to her tummy area. Did that cause the bleeding that killed her? Despite every doctor reassuring me that I hadn't killed my mom, that thought haunted me for months. I didn't tell many people I was experiencing these feelings and those I did confide in downplayed my feelings or dismissed me. My brother, for example, callously told me to "forget it and move on" like it was nothing. Invalidated, traumatized and burnt out, my addiction became extreme.

Before I knew it, the things that I didn't lose naturally, I lost from my drinking. My marriage took a huge hit as both of us were drinking heavily. The consequences of our alcoholism manifested differently for the two of us and we both did horrible things. Unfortunately, my manifestations always came out in fits of rage and anger at the world and everyone around me. I was a pressure cooker. My addiction released a monster that was dormant in me. That monster was just waiting for me to drink so he could come out and release all the pent-up negative emotions, emotions that I could have dealt with better had I gone to grief therapy or counseling.

Ultimately, I was able to convince my husband to get help for his drinking. He had gotten to the point where he had nearly gotten us killed on more than one occasion and his family had connections with a very successful rehab facility. Ultimately, we worked together and got him into rehab. When he was improving and released, he saw that I too was in severe need of help. I was constantly drunk and surely that was not good for his recovery. I was having inappropriate outbursts at people, and not my normal self whatsoever. Unfortunately, he didn't sit me down, hold my hand and get me into rehab, like I did him. Instead, he cowardly fled under the cover of dark, with his parents, and never spoke to me again. He saw that I was sick and in desperate need of help and instead of helping me, his partner for 12 years, most of them AMAZING, he left. Not only did he leave a 12 year relationship like it was nothing, he got a restraining order, had me thrown out into the streets and literally left to die. I truly almost did.

Suddenly, I found myself, homeless and broke with basically nothing. The only belongings I had left were my car and my dog. That didn't last long either. Before I knew it, I had gotten two DUI's in two different states in two days back to back… bye bye car. Oh, and then my dog died. In 2 years I literally lost EVERYTHING, some by life's terms and other's on alcohol's terms.

At that point I knew I had to check into rehab but before I could my brother had me involuntarily committed. He claims that he sectioned me because he "knew I would check myself out" of the traditional rehab I wanted to go to. My rebuttal is that I never provided him with any evidence of this. I was cuffed, shackled, stripped of my belongings, my freedom and essentially placed in prison for three months.

I am grateful for the healing that came along with my brother's actions but still struggle with having my freedom, choices and autonomy taken away from me, for many reasons. Reading his petition to the judge was probably one of the worst things I've ever experienced in my life. Still, it paved the road for me to get into alcohol detox, treatment and recovery. My journey to healing began on that day.

Many of you reading this have been through similar experiences. You may have lost loved ones due to death, separation or divorce. You may have experienced trauma that was unbearable, betrayal that was unfathomable. You may have coped in all the wrong ways, using drugs or alcohol to drum out the pain. You may have tried to hide your use from your peers despite the fact that they already knew something was wrong. You may have bottled up all of your emotions until, while under the influence, you blew up for no good reason at the smallest thing. You may have done terrible things that you would otherwise never do. You may have lied, stolen, cheated. You may have been incarcerated or exposed to legal trouble, "caught some cases".

If you are reading this, it is not too late. You still haven't found yourself in a cemetery. You may have come close, but there is still hope. Recovery is possible and I am living proof that we can get better despite any odds thrown our way. I hope you can relate to some of this poetry, moreover I hope that it inspires you to find some healthy coping mechanisms of your own, like art, poetry or music. I hope my work helps you to commit to your own recovery and your own success. It is possible.

A NOTE ABOUT RESOURCES

It's never easy admitting that you have a substance abuse problem, but you are not alone at all. If you are willing to acknowledge that your life has become unmanageable and ask for help there are limitless resources out there just waiting to help. Assistance with food, housing, long term treatment, clothing, physical and mental health care and more is out there for you.

If you are the concerned about a family member or loved one, you too are not alone. There are many resources available for you to utilize in your effort to get that person the help they need.

The following hotline resources are also free, confidential, and available 24/7:

DrugAbuse.com hotline: (888) 966-8152

Addiction Navigators on call 24/7 to help answer any questions related to drug abuse and support

Al-Anon and Ala-teen hotline line: 800-356-9996 – Counselors provide support to teens and adults who are negatively impacted by alcohol addiction and provide resources to group therapy nearby for ongoing support.

Substance Abuse and Mental Health Services Administration (SAMHSA): 1-800-662-4357 – English/Spanish speaking counselors provide referrals to treatment facilities, support groups, and community-based services.

National Suicide Prevention: 1-800-273-8255 – Support to help those in crisis process their emotional distress and prevent suicide.

Boys Town: 1-800-448-3000 – Over 140 languages can be translated; they also provide a telecommunications device for the deaf (TDD) line for the speech and hearing impaired (1-800-448-1833).

Drugfree.org: call 855-378-4373 or text 55753 – Counselors provide support and education and guide you to the best course of action.

A NOTE ABOUT THE POETRY

As human beings we all go through similar experiences. Each poem in this book was written in the hopes that you, the reader, can relate to it and maybe find some comfort and motivation with the realization that you are not alone in your experiences.

A NOTE ABOUT THE POETRY

PART ONE:
TRAUMA, GRIEF AND LOSS

TRAUMA

It's like a fingerprint
or strand of DNA
unique to you
individual
sure, others will relate
empathize
some may even sympathize
but your pain is your experience
and your grief manifests
uniquely to you
and it hurts
and for what it's worth
I KNOW it hurts
but don't drink the strychnine
and expect others to die
don't punish yourself
expecting to punish the pain.

EXSANGUINATION

I'm bleeding out
a crimson flood
exsanguinating
losing blood
you tore out my heart
dropped it with a thud
kicked it around
bacteria filled mud.

I languish now
lethargic and existing
solace overwhelms
and intimidates me
a grain of sand
caught in an oyster…
will this experience
reinvigorate me,
the wound you created
obliterates me,
the death of our marriage
incinerates me….

I miss you so much….it incinerates me.

ALL WE EVER WANTED

All we ever wanted
we had yet threw away
I shouldn't have been drinking
when you returned from rehab that day.
All I ever needed
was to lay there on your chest
and listen to your heart lub dub
as we'd blend and rest
but you left

Now I hear you packed up all my shit in such a drastic way
said you loved me then abandoned me in a single day
might have met another but he'll never ever be MK
I'll be okay
I'll always love you Greg
even though you threw it all away

MISSING YOU

I'm not dreaming of you each night
waking up in terror and sweats.
I'm not tossing and turning each night
in a sea filled with many regrets
I'm not….I'm not.

Because if I keep on telling myself this
maybe it'll come to fruition
I'm not exactly in
fantastic condition
if I keep on telling myself
that I'm not missing…
YOU
then maybe I'm not
I'm not
in continuous shock
in shock that you left me
I'm not…. I'm not
thinking you detest me
that our entire existence just suddenly stopped
I'm not…. I'm not

    and that's the consequence of this traveling circus
    I just can't believe you'd fucking desert us
    disposed of me as if I were worthless….
    (I'm not…. I'm not)
    I'm so sorry for my role but I didn't deserve THIS!

So NO I don't miss you and NO I don't care,
I DON'T grab onto my pillow pretending you're there
NO I'm not locked up in a 35 section
with everyone saying that this is a blessing
I'm not sitting here completely obsessing
that I'm not…. I'm not
WITH YOU

LIFE ENDS TOO SOON

I loved you so much I couldn't decide

If I would have enough strength or melt down as I cried

5 other men right by my side

escorting you and saying goodbye

and the cold metal bar would slide from my grip

going up those stairs convinced I would trip

embarrassing to all but mostly to you

you carried me through life, you carried me through

So how does one find

the strength to pall bear

carrying you

when you're not at all there

while you're shining on down

with your heavenly rays

we beg for the strength

to get through the dark days.

Jesus, dear Jesus, my lord and my savior

forgive all my sins and outrageous behavior

help me forgive others and follow your will

do well by my peers and remember you still

carry them now when life's in it's bloom

instead of a coffin-

life ends too soon

LOVE DOES NOT STOP

True love

Real love

Comes by rarely

And when you find it

Hold on tightly

Never let go

Fight for it

Make compromises

Communicate

Always say I love you

Before going to bed

Wake up in the morning

And look at them

And know

How special you have it

Love

Hold on to it tightly

Fight for it

And cherish it

Forever

HEAVILY FOR YOU

I wish you were here

cause last night I cried

I know you would have wrapped me in something warm

and asked for spiders

you know, that little way I'd tickle you gently

creating the sensation of little legs

and snore and hog the sheets

and I'd love it all

I listened to "Someone Like You" from Adele last night

powerful song

I know these planets spin spin spin

and that we all have a path

but when it comes time to put my head on my pillow

I realize how alone I feel without you

I will never stop loving you- with my passionate broken heart

and though I will carry on and live and love again

I know exactly where my regrets are

Coping was easier when on that barstool

than dealing with everything.

When I next fall in love

I will have learned from all those mistakes

I know I am not the only person who cries

but these tears still fall heavily for you

FOUR CHAMBERS AND TEARS

When your suddenly faced with facing your fears

when you can finally release what you've hidden for years

when you tell them to listen but they just cannot hear

you learn to grow and move on

When you just want forgiveness, but he says he can't give it

When you lose sleep at night cause you always relive it

when it's tragic and closure's not an option, just isn't

you learn to say sorry and move on

When you take someone's innocence and murder their heart

when you're constantly wishing you could go back to the start

when you realize you're at fault for it falling apart

you need to forgive and move on

When the thing I want most is no longer here

When there's days that our purpose in life isn't clear

if you can't forgive me, I'll just disappear

cause there's more that's involved than four chambers and tears

CHRISTMAS WITHOUT YOU

Somewhere inside your inside

yet outside your heart

music, dancing, drinking, and juice

empty pill bottles

from the meds that you used

kings and professors

the scribes and the proctors

document life

and it's pitfalls like doctors

dip deeper into life, make it happen

even when your bed feels better

even when the odds and circumstances

are piled against you

you know you are better

put on your glitter

sneakers not shoes

and dance till you sweat, smile till it hurts, laugh till it's better

tin foil, and napkins

he hurt you- then slap him

he wronged you, just ask him

should I be filled with hate and aggression

after the nights I stayed up late with depression

tossing and turning with worries and questions

denaturing and so I detest him

the tree and the lights go up

as the snow falls down

jingle bells ring

EVEN IF IT HURTS A LOT

Even if it hurts a lot

if we fix these wounds

or maybe not,

even if this breaks my heart,

if my decisions

are so fucking far from smart

even if we can't go back

if we knock our fucking train off track

if the world hates us and we hate them back

if my broken heart has a heart attack

and even if we both find peace

if we separate, and embrace our release

if they go against all of our beliefs

we need to feel a bit of relief:

worlds die around us

the rest of our lives

is happening as we speak

seeing your name on my phone leaves me weak

I sacrifice my pride and image and life for remission

here's to hoping

here's to wishing

I GAVE YOU AN OUT

I gave you an out, opened the door

said I'll understand, if you wanted no more

I gave you an out, but you lied to me

said you wanted to stay, got me to believe

I gave you an out

and you just played a game

fucked up my heart

fucked up my name

I gave you an out

and you showed your true self

turned love into hate

this hurts like hell.

I had no more pain meds,

no shots, no refills

just gave you my heart

paint on your easel

but you fucking lied

you're cold and you're evil

I gave you an out

but you didn't take it, you didn't need to

let me drive you all around, sucked my money, safe and sound, called me names,

beat me to the ground

, jealous, jealous, tore us down

I had faults, caused some fights, but apologized, and made things right

I didn't deserve how you brought this about

when I gave you goodbye, I gave you an out.

Deep in the Dimension of Halo's and Wings
(We will be together again one day)

Deep in the dimension of halo's and wings,
there's majestic, and golden, and beautiful things,
there's mansions, with meadows, and willowing trees,
there's freedom, and rainbows, and sweet memories,
there are elf with night-sashes, and inside them is glitter,
old pets and new pets with the rest of their litter,
there's magic, and top hats, and ruby's that talk,
mobile units in the valleys so you don't have to walk,
there's banquets, abundant, with fruit and red wine,
there's an apple in the mouth of fire roasted swine,
goblets with no bottoms, dinnerware that can fly
you never say "sorry", "miss you" or "goodbye"
you go wherever you imagine yourself to be
you're as large as a mountain but as small as a flea
you can't help but smile as the music infuses
everyone is a champion and nobody loses,
children run laughing, and wise ones observe,
there's scrolls with the poetry you thought no one heard,
there's dragons almighty, who breathe fire and ice
but none of them chase you cause they're all super nice,
there's Gods, and there's thunder, and there's rods of pure light,
you're refreshed every morning, cause you sleep well at night,
cats roam with dogs and livestock in the streets,
there's servants who dress you and provide the clean sheets...
Everyone that you've loved, that got taken too soon,
wait for you there in a tremendous ballroom,
and I know that one day, I'll open my eyes, and see the majestic, and golden sunrise,
I'll be in a mansion, watching Flagyl outside, and I'll breath super deep, as tears rush to my eyes,
I'll be in a bowtie, in a fancy tuxedo, and I'll play with him fondly in a willow filled meadow,
I'll run to that ballroom, I'll call out for Stacey, you'll be right in the center, you'll turn and you'll face me,
all white, and with diamonds, with those beautiful eyes, and I'll drop to my knees, with overjoyed cries,
I'll try to say "sorry" but you hold out your hand, I'll try to say "I missed you" but you help me to stand,
I'll say that I love you, and I'll love you forever, then we play in the thunder and lightning together,
we'll be joined by our loved ones, as everyone sings,
deep in the dimension of halo's and wings...

CLEATS

I'm wearing cleats!
Why did you leave?
You left me to fend for myself in the streets.

You were a wreck.
I was one too.
It manifested differently for me and for you.

BUT I GOT YOU HELP
despite all you did
but when I needed HELP you left and you hid.

You ruined my life,
not just a slice,
burnt me to the ground without thinking twice.

12 fucking years.
12 fucking years.
You vanished and left me homeless in tears.

You knew me better than anyone. You knew I needed help. I knew you did….and got
you into treatment. But when you got better and came home to me, a vulnerable,
nervously broken down and medicated me…..you left. You didn't talk to me. You didn't
even try to have a conversation. We didn't even get closure and for that I suffer
eternally. Was I so bad you couldn't talk to me before restraining me? Met someone
else and just find it easier to decapitate us. Did the decade of good times mean
nothing? Nothing?

I'm now wearing cleats,
won't be dragged through the streets,
no one, ever again
will bring me to my knees
I've come to believe
that God made you leave
in order to preserve my own sanity.

COLLATERAL DAMAGE

Armed back to back
we stood with our weapons drawn
"United Front" we said
so we aimed and we pointed
at all of our demons
one by one we shot them down
beating the odds,
but those demons grew
in speed and number,
we fought harder
and harder
grabbing tighter and tighter
onto our triggers
and as we continued to fight
you turned to the left I turned to the right
we fought for forever
we fought day and night
still the demons kept coming
from the cover of night
you turned more to the left, me more to the right….
it got so overwhelming,
surrounded and tight
bruised, we kept shielding
each dark demon bite
fighting an insurmountable fight
further we turned
to the left; to the right
until we were facing each other
and couldn't unite…
pulling the trigger
without a goodbye
I'll love you forever
we fought the good fight

GOODBYE

That moment

that instant

they draw their last breath

your so spent

your distant

and you'll never forget

the feeling

sensation

when that tear starts to form

your standing

so calmly

amidst one perfect storm

I'm lost

and I'm lonely

without your impact

and the truth

of the matter

is a matter

of fact

there's nothing so powerful

as that tear in your eye

and there's nothing so hard

as saying goodbye

EVERY GREY SKY BREAKS TO THE SUN
(There are people who love you and they will help you through this)

It's never easy without explanation
days get so bad you can't help but hate them
watching your loved ones
watching them cry
saying I'm sorry
saying goodbye
but every grey sky breaks to the sun
things will improve for everyone
every dark cloud often make rain
but after we cry- we WILL smile again
there are really no words I can give to console you
when emotions of grief and sadness control you
I'll pray this time passes, you're strong and I know you
you're wise and the Lord will find ways to console you
cause every grey sky breaks to the sun
and I'm blessed to have found such a special someone
you were there for me when I had no one
I love you my friend-
just wait for the sun.....

LAMENTATION

It's 4am
and I'd rather be sleeping
my Folgers decaf tea is steeping
I think of u while continuously weeping
this whole thing's so hard to digest.

It's 4:03
and I'm tossing and turning
my English muffin smells good but it's burning
it's hard living life without you but I'm learning
to live with this pain in my chest.

It's 4:05
and my headache is throbbing
watched Cassie and Cole, my weeping turned sobbing
I miss you so much; this pain is alarming
my heart is filled with distress.

It's now 4:10
every minute is boring
I wish you were right on the side of me snoring
you were my favorite excuse to sleep in every morning
your cuddles were always the best

No matter the second, the minute, or hour
life without you is bitter and sour
the swiss cheese on your legs that we would devour
is gone now, and I cannot rest

Your memory Is the only thing holding me here
you kept me together, your messy little queer,
my insides are screaming, I miss you my dear,
A life without u- I detest

Castles have crumbled, Foundations have bent
Oceans have emptied, Angels lament
I wish I just knew where the fuck you went
I'll love u long past my dying breath

TUG OF WAR

TUG OF WAR

One hand in the future
One reaching back
One hand extended
One losing grasp
Pullin and stretchin
In every direction
Trying to hold on to my past

And the rope tears my skin
Corrosive, abrading
As my future is forming
My past is fading
The force of the current
In the waters I'm wading
Is almost too strong
Obliterating

I hoped he would comeback
Somehow return
I held on to that rope
So tight it would burn
And despite all my wishes
And how much I've yearned
There's one goddamn lesson
I've finally learned….

It's time to let go

PART TWO:
LGBTQIA/SEXUALITY

UNDERSTANDING MYSELF

She didn't work so I tried him on for size

and he didn't fit, the inseam was too tight

and now I find myself in between, in a limbo state

the taste is almost sexy, the feeling's almost great

I love her hands upon my chest

and his stubble on my skin

I love my rapid heart beat

I tremble deep within

I love this strong attraction

when I'm looking in their eyes

I love the control I take

when I move my own just right

as the smoke and fog settle

and the music starts to beat

I find myself tasting them

as they sweat from all this heat

and with each drop of water

beading off their necks

I dance right in between them

her body, his soul

are wrecks

all three dancers strangers

whom do I prefer

to kiss and leave the dance floor with

is it him or her?

VENOM

Try it
feel, feel, feel it
your arms and your legs and fingers go dead
and your eyes, they get glossy
rolling back in your head
the feeling is wicked
it pierces but soothes
blood cells like the red sea
part, making room
one light flickering
cat claws and moans
pornography on
so shut off your phone
handcuffs, netting
sweat drops and groans
dripping, just dripping
in juices and foam

I can't hear you
over revving of engines
but I feel your heartbeat
all your injections
push past that ugly limit
dig your fingernails deeply
and go further into the glimmer
push past the heat and into the beach
push past the skin and into the vein
and then push and then push
find your spotlight on the dance floor
know which dirty corner is yours at two
when there's nothing between you and your lover
its paralytic; your tongue
silence push pull punch spit
until waves of some bouncer calling out
surface to your ears,
you smell differently now that your sweat and cologne
and part of your spirit are mixed with mine
like oysters and wine
like hell mixed with heaven
like Satin and Jesus
like water, like venom

DISCOVER

Oh Jesus, dear Jesus
please show me direction
he's a messy, distasteful
opportunistic infection
whenever he'd call
I'd just drop to the floor
but now I delete, or push on ignore
and whenever we'd contact
I'd be hoping for answers
but instead he kept killing
our love like a cancer
and though I'm still sad
I'm just thrilled to recover
there's more to this world
I'm destined to discover

CALL ME EASY

Call me easy, call me a whore
it's not my fault they always want more
call me crazy an emotional ride
but they get on and off (multiple times)
call me jealous, leave me in distress,
leave me for dead, leave me a mess....
you say you don't want this
but then you get pissed
if you think there's another,
is there something I missed?
I'll overcome this and only get stronger
won't stoop to the lows that I did any longer
cause I'm not a yo-yo riding your string
say what you want, keep gossiping
I wanted forgiveness
I kept reaching and grabbing
while you and your parents
were busy backstabbing
so call me easy
call me a whore
just do me a favor
don't call me anymore

YEAH

It's a million degrees and about to get hotter.

Body secretions all over my parlor.

The red lights are on, the sirens alarming

I'm doing much better since I lost "prince charming"

and on May nineteenth I'm donating my body

to the devil himself for a steaming hot party.

I'm lighting a fire hotter than hell

I hope to make secrets that I'll never tell

surrounded by people I know can throw down

I don't care if it's busy or if no one's around

I'll be with my best friends on roof decks with drinks

then out on the dance floor with meatheads and twinks

Mariah and Miley and even some Kesha

it's gonna be blazing, I'm willing to bet ya

PEEP SHOW

We can do it in the back while they're playing our song

leave the door open a crack, it's what they've wanted all along

you know they all like it, them horny ass gays

they'll watch as I bite it, in all sorts of ways

so let's put on a peep show, make 'em all watch

make em get sweaty, excited and hard

let's put on a peep show for all to observe

they'll hang on our actions, on our every word

let's give them a second where they finally see

how hot it can get between you and me

let's give them a peep show, rip off my shirt

it won't feel as hot unless you make it hurt

kiss on my lips and then kiss on my neck

hands moving restlessly, they won't forget

give them a second to just comprehend

how fucking well our bodies can blend

and just when I've pinned you, you muster up strength

to push me up backwards, we go to all lengths

clothes flying off in every direction

each boy in the background has a full on erection

and just when we get to the point where we fuck

we slam the door hard, "good night boys, good luck"

SEX

There's a thrill in knowing that nobody knows

a game that you're playing behind doors that are closed...

So as soon as we close them I kiss on your mouth

please be relentless and push me about

we rub as we undress and go up the stairs

but we stumble a bit, our thoughts are elsewhere

and finally there's nothing between us but skin

we sigh and we moan and we grab and we grin

my sensors are up you're calling my name

still nobody knows we're playing this game

so we pause for a moment to gather some breath

you reach for a candle we're fully undressed

my body feels broken so I ask you to fix it

use me as your token to be masochistic

we wrestle a moment and soon it goes down

slower then faster and soon off the ground

a rocket can't blast off if you give it no heat

we're tossing and turning and biting the sheets

they sweat from the action beads of my mouth

I want you to taste it, too breathless to shout

so I look in your eyes now as we move toward our goal

you feel it I feel it, our bodies just flow

and soon comes a climax, we feel it together

nails down my back just make it feel better

and when it is over we kiss and we mend

regain our composure then start up again

there's a thrill in knowing that nobody knows

a game that you're playing behind doors that are closed

KEEP ON YOUR RING

Some boys don't know their place in the club, looking for romance, looking for love.
They look for fulfillment, until it turns two, look for completion, but what can you do?
I'm so not that guy, I just wanna dance, and at the end of the night, I'll get in your pants.
Give me a strobe light, give me a chance, give me the grip of your strong working hands
give me a reason to be up in your shit, dance till we sweat, and then give me it
glitter and scents and sights, touching skin, finding a hottie and flirting with him
drum beats, heart beats, beats beats beats, I'm beauty, power and salt and the rhythm
magnetic, electric, offensive when with him
I'll take off my clothes I'll be sorta nasty, I'll do magic things with my hips if you ask me
I'm sexy and scandal and grapes from the vine, killer green eyes, a smile that is kind
and dude, really, don't take off your ring it feels fucking hot when it's rubbing against me
muscles and sweat and poppers and kissing, all of this time, this is what I was missing?
So when the drum beats I expect you can move, in time with the music, in time with my
groove
if she's waiting at home, we'll go to my crib, no one has to ever know what we did
biting, and gripping spitting and dripping
soaking each other and the sheets of the bedding
breaking all of the vows from your wedding
using your tongue as mine for sheer pleasure
we're like hunters or vampires when we are together
and after we're finished, get dressed and go home
from now on I'm sleeping in MY bed ALONE
you're fun when it's club time, you got the right potion
but I'm not looking for love, a date or devotion

911

Call 911
just get to a phone
and call 911
I'm in rehab alone
get me a fireman
say there's a fire
he'll use his big hose
to quench my desires
Call 911
say there's a murder!
The'll send a detective
I hope he's a squirter!
Call 911
SCREAM "HEART ATTACK"
paramedics will cum
I'll make em cum fast
So tell them it's arson
say there's a crime
I need a hot body
buried in mine
I need an emergent
load in my bum
call me a whore
just call 911

HOMOPHOBIA

They're so homophobic and they don't even know it

Innate and passive hate, they cannot control it

'tolerance'- A minimalist approach to hatred

I don't want to be tolerated

I don't want to be put up with

It equates to being degraded

I spent so long suppressed no wonder I was depressed

Trying to please the world with how I looked and how I dressed

They say that God condemns; we'll go to hell when this world ends

But the God I pray to doesn't hate he's one of my best friends

I don't take your life and overanalyze

I don't dissect your every move so please don't dissect mine

Take your fucking microscope and examine your own shit

Two faced, over-critical I just can't deal with it

I'm back, my view is so improved I'm free from so much strife

and those who bring bad energy are stricken from my life

All the choices that I made, the sins I would commit

I paid for by losing everything and now I'm done with it

My life and world are revived, redeemed, no matter your point of view

I'm done with names like drama queen, the biggest mess is you

Someone I met the other day equated gay with cancer

But no treatment that could be prescribed

Could beat this night club dancer

SIPS OF DELIVERANCE

(My Godfather passed a few years back, we never got to talk about me being gay)

I see a mountain and you there waving
I'm reaching for you in deep need of saving
drowning and fighting so I swim to survive
I'm so deep in this ocean while you're way up high
and they put the tourniquet a little too tight
I'm bleeding and bleeding and bleeding tonight
at the end I'll be left with a large hematoma
lost in a daze, an sweet induced coma
lost in a dream, where I finally reached you
I'm lost and I'm crying and I desperately need you

Dear Uncle Don
godfather and friend
I'm reaching the line
I'm reaching the end
and I pray and I pray and a ask for an angel
I never forgot, betrayed or renamed you
I turned to some things that just weren't right
but those things are over and I need you tonight
I wish you could see how far that I've come
I turned myself into a successful someone
and still on the bright days, it feels just like rain
tears, empty bottles, no answers just pain
and I know you're up there, just sitting with meme
laughing and talking about back in the day
but I just need a sign, cause I so fucking miss you
I'm crying out loud, and there's no fucking tissues
why in the fuck did he take your lungs
you were my friend and you were so young
and although I got distant, it was just out of fear
that you might not understand my life over here
but I miss when you'd walk in with a big case of beer
birthday cakes from Carvelle, magician sets every year
you knew I wanted to make magic.....
and I did.

Now I just wish you were here to talk cause I'm feeling pretty broken.... and I miss you

ROCK ME TO SLEEP

It's ten in the evening and the Earth simply hums
I'm in my little corner of the world with someone
we rent nightly movies; watch "don't the trust the b"
everything's perfect when you're next to me
Hearing you breathe, when you're lying with me
rocks me to sleep, darling, it rocks me to sleep

I ask you to scratch my left upper back
to tickle my neck and do spiders.
The story of my life and all of it's details
has really just never been brighter
the feeling I feel when we cuddle at night
is like being sung to and rocked by the fire
and Moxy finds comfort as she lay by our feet
all curled up with her chew toy beside her.
Rock me to sleep, my sweet phoenix rock me to sleep

I love you're big muscles, you're beautiful smile;
I love all your little surprises and when we drift off at the end of the night
a force-field materializes nothing can hurt us, nothing can break my will,
my love, my vision or hope I'll love and protect you till the day that I die,
and then after when I am a ghost
and believe me, forever,
I'll rock you to sleep, I love you,
I'll rock you to sleep

DISMEMBER

Take my feet- there's no use dancing, if there's no running to you,
take my feet- take my feet.

Take my hands- if I can't hold yours then I have nothing left to hold on to
your wish is my command, take my hands- take my hands

Take my voice- I can't sing without you- the notes come out wrong,
my love's a conviction and it was never a choice- so take my voice- take my voice

Take my ears- just take both my ears- there's nothing I'll listen to- nothing I wanna hear-
just take these ears, just take my ignorant ears.

Take both my arms- they're no use to me- if I cannot hug you- I'm not where I'm meant
to be- it's such cruelty- take these arms- take em both from me.

Remove these lips- these lips of mine- when there's no hope left of u being mine- I won't
kiss another like I used to kiss you- so take these lips from this silly fool.

And these green eyes of mine- please take them too- they're useless and blinded if I
can't see you- so take them both- these beautiful eyes-
this way I can't cry,
just pluck out my eyes

Just take all of me-
take every part-
you've already stolen my soul and my heart-
now everything else might as well go too-
you're my only love
my angel, my boo…

DON'T TELL MAMA

Don't tell my mama that you and I date,
She'll just throw a tantrum and get all irate.
Then you'll have to sneak out the window again.
No more broken bones

There's sand on my feet I'm driving in sandals.
I smell like sun lotion, Corona, and scandal!
The waves pummeled us like we were rag dolls.
And whenever you touch me I get more aroused

Swimming in saltwater is like swimming in tears.
I don't want to cry so don't say we were here.
Don't tell my mama that we're sneaking around.
She'll pick up a blender and chase you abound,
as you're running you'll tell her she's being unfair
but she's throwing utensils and good silverware.

Screaming so much you can't even decipher.
Most of the words that come from inside her:
"Hell is place that's for real don't you know?
It's where all of the boys who like boys have to go
It's the place you we're destined to go since when born
Deep in The Dimension of Pitchforks and Horns"

Carnival lights and musical sounds
balloons from the mouth of water gun clowns
We get to the top of the Ferris wheel ride
It pauses a moment to let folks inside
our carriage rocks and you steal a kiss
it's a moment of time filled with absolute bliss

Innocence fading with little explosions
I wanna have time to explore and to know him
So please, I hope my mom never knows
You know what kind of tantrums she throws
And you'll just become someone that I must avoid
She'll tell me that good boys don't like other boys
She'll threaten to get my papa involved
And I'll end up on back of a milk carton somehow
She'll ground me again and lock me up tight
Force me to sneak out your window each night….
No more broken bones

ALL CAUSE HE DIDN'T FIT IN

Sullen and lonely, he wakes every morning and clumsily falls out of bed.
He has plans to wake up at six and eat breakfast but he always oversleeps instead.
He looks in the mirror and vigorously runs his fingers through his starchy blonde hair
but despite his technique and a whole lot of gel, there's one cluster that stays in the air.
He gets to his school about ten minutes late and scurries the halls before class.
He gets to his desk when the teacher is talking and drops all his books like an ass.
He's the target of all the bullies in school cause he's waifish with coke bottle specs.
They laugh and point fingers and whisper behind him and steal all his answers to tests.
But on June 6 at six in the evening the skies grew unusually dark.
All of his curtains drew themselves closed and his door automatically locked.
Smoke filled his room and he on his bed was stilled with both fear and surprise.
He couldn't believe what then happened next in front of his blurry blue eyes.
A man in a suit of impeccable style Black Gucci, with a matching black vest.
His tie and the trimmings including the cuff links were all a hypnotizing red.
He approached with a snarl that was almost a grin, you wouldn't believe what he said.
The following morning the alarm clock went off he stretched and rolled out of bed.
Tempted to make tons of bacon with breakfast he got on the treadmill instead.
He looked in the mirror and effortlessly styled his hair with a popular trend.
And he knew in his heart based on his reflection he'd have no problem making friends.
He gets to his school early enough to socialize a bit before class
He gets to his desk before lecture starts and everyone checks out his ass.
The bullies avoid him cause he's tougher than them and the girls simply fall at his feet.
He gets a hall pass to make out in the bathroom, passing tests without having to cheat.
But on June 6 at six in the evening this boy made a deal laced with sin.
Gave his soul to the devil in exchange for some luck; A man in a suit with a grin.
And now that life's over, he grinds and he wails.
All cause he didn't fit in!

PART THREE:
SUBSTANCE USE

DEEPER

Deeper and deeper
I go deeper and deeper
getting deeper and deeper
in the hole.

The debts that I'm owing
are constantly growing
while I just sit here knowing
there's so many I owe.

Deeper and deeper
I go deeper and deeper
getting deeper and deeper
in the hole.

The shit that I'm drinking
fucks up my thinking
so I keep on sinking
I know

Deeper and deeper
I go deeper and deeper
getting deeper and deeper
in the hole.

BACK IN THE CLOSET

Sitting here sectioned
the big 35
my twin brother did it
"to keep me alive".
It's designed like a prison
and filled with all guys
many ex cons
with hate in their eyes
it's supposed to be rehab
we're encouraged to share
but how can I do that
with THEM sitting there?
How can I sit here
and profess my own truth
when I can't say "my HUSBAND"
"I'm GAY" or name you?
How can I process
all of this trauma
when I can't show expression
the way that I wanna?

CONSEQUENSES HAVE CONSEQUENSES

It started slowly, surreptitious,
dinner and drinks
oysters and wine
slowly we are conditioned
(I was)
to associate our usage with solace
comfort, consolation,
absolution.

Rough shift at work? "Let's go for drinks!"
It's the weekend? "Let's go for drinks!"
Vacation? Weddings? Funerals? Parties?
"Time to let loose and relax!"
Many cultures insist on serving alcohol with most meals.
It's glorified in the media,
accepted, standardized, normalized, embraced.
THIS IS AN ILLUSION
It's not normal, it's poison
all chemicals are poison
for your body and your mind,
and sooner or later, it WILL catch up to you and drag you down.
You see, if you eventually come to depend on substances
to relax, calm down, grieve, or escape it's already too late.

Consequences have consequences!
The consequence of alcohol and drug use is a change in your behavior,
you can get slower, or faster, weakened or slurred…unsteady.
You can grow angry or loving, horny or unable to perform….
you might drive, hurt someone, hurt yourself….. kill.
And the consequences of these behaviors can be catastrophic.

STUMBLE

Have you ever been so drunk
sideways walking
blurred vision
cross eyed
spitting
accidentally in the eyes
of those you're bullshitting?
Saying all the wrong things
cause you've lost inhibitions,
doing the wrong things,
bad decisions?
You might get obnoxious
as time passes by
or loving or mean
or attempt to drive.

I've stumbled,
I've stumbled,
I've done all those things,
dove into that vodka
and the trouble it brings
gone from monosyllabic
to social, to a mess
to clumsily dancing
and anonymous sex
I've stolen moms pills
from the drawer in her desk
I've shot up so much
my veins are a mess.
I destroyed all my friendships
my family, my marriage,
burnt life to the ground
a bloody miscarriage.

Prevention is the best way to treat a disease.
Today is the best day to stand tall and STAY CLEAN!

MONSTEROUS HANDS

These monstrous hands aren't the hands of a monster,
these hands belong to a man!
They have helped people heal
to stand, to walk, to run.
They have helped provide
bring comfort
make change
and even bring new life into this world.
They have linked fingers tightly
as loved ones and patients have passed on.

These monstrous hands aren't the hands of a monster, but there is a monster within,
they have turned through the pages of the King James bible
they have caressed a lover's skin
these hands tremble cause they couldn't handle it all
when things weren't ideal or swell
so they grabbed onto a bottle of alcohol
and it clawed my drunk ass into hell

These monstrous hands aren't the hands of a monster,
but there's a monster inside me I think.
He lays there dormant
patiently
in wait
until I pick up a drink.

MORE

I'll just go get 3 nips this morning
as soon as the liquor store unlocks their doors
just to stop the shakes
tomorrow I'll only have two
the next day one
then I'll be done.

Hold up, hold up,
did I already drink all 3?
I seriously drank all of them?
Oh boy, I'll just get 2 more
as soon as I pass another liquor store.

Wait.... why just get 2 more?
I bet they have a minimum spending limit for my card anyway!
I'll get 5 more,
I go through them so quickly.

The world is spinning and spinning. I can't stand or walk straight.
I think I am speaking clearly but everyone says my speech is slurred.
I think that I can see clear enough but notice my vision is blurred.

Vikings, apostles, philosophers and scribes
prophets, precogs and chiefs,
couldn't tell me how I ever survived
my drinking was beyond belief.

A SWISH, A SWALLOW AND A CHASE

I am fucked up
I lost it all
so effortlessly
with the twist of a cap
a swish, a swallow and a chase.

Round and round I then go
faster faster, slower till slow
a dazed, glazed, zombie slur
unaware
waking up in strange places
on the side of strange bodies
unfamiliar faces
I do risky things
that my mind erases

all with the twist of a cap
a swish, a swallow and a chase.

HOUSE OF MIRRORS

I'm stuck
I'm trapped
I'm lost
with no map
I can't even go back
cause I'm stuck
and I'm trapped

I'm spinning
I'm spinning
in a house full of mirrors
wishing my vision
would get a bit clearer
my reflection surrounds me
it's drawing in nearer
forced to confront
the demons I fear.
They torture my mind
all of the time
I'm seeking atonement
for behaviors of mine
so many people
to whom I was unkind
fear me or are happy
to leave me behind

I'm stuck
I'm trapped
wish I could go back
surrounded by mirrors
it's such a bitch slap
all of my demons
wrapped up in gift wrap
but I'll face and defeat this, I'll break all this glass
and be free.

HISSY FITS

Hissy fits
Hissy fits
sometimes I scream
and clench both my fists
I can be such a child
a winy little bitch
stomping my feet
I become frantic
I might hold my breath
till I'm blue in the lips
take something whole
and shred it to bits
cause when I'm upset
I don't give two shits
I start to lash out
and act like a prick
I don't like myself
when acting like this
hissy fits
hissy fits.

CADILLAC PUNCH BUGGY

Cadillac punch buggy
poisonous snakes
dilated pupils
I still have the shakes
The enormity I experience
endorses earthquakes!
The osmosis considers my destiny
for putting some booze in him and the rest in me
God! so many people detesting me
police chasing and arresting me
it just sorta occurred
my speech got slurred
my behavior spiraling
becoming absurd
I'm a freaking alcoholic
or haven't you heard???
It's time to summons the best in me!

PART FOUR:
DETOX, TREATMENT AND RECOVERY

WHAT IS A SECTION 35

Section 35 is a Massachusetts law that allows a qualified person to request a court order requiring someone to be civilly committed and treated involuntarily for an alcohol or substance use disorder. This can be a spouse, a loved one, a policeman or judge. You can even section yourself if you genuinely acknowledge that you need help. If your drug or alcohol use is putting yourself or others at risk, a court can remove you from your current living situation and place you into a rehabilitation or correctional facility against your will. Length of stay varies but usually ranges from 1-3 months.

My estranged brother had me sectioned. Even though I was literally on my way to rehab, he insisted on taking my entire existence into his own hands. I was abducted from my life, cuffed, shackled, thrown into a police wagon and violently transported to what equated to a prison for three months. Admittedly, there I received the help I needed. I will forever be grateful for that. But like many of us who have been sectioned, I am so angry at him for taking away my choice, especially because I had already committed to doing it on my own. He claimed to have done it because he "knew I would check out of any rehab prematurely" but he had zero evidence of that. Despite me begging him in the halls of the court to let me do it myself, he refused, and proceeded to present the judge with an entire dossier about my behavior. I was denied my own right to check into a rehab for the first time in my life.

When I was discharged I was given a copy of my brother's court petition for section 35. Reading it literally took away some of my soul, it actually killed what was left of our already fractured and flailing "relationship". Sure, there were things in there that were factual and I claim responsibility for what I did to hurt people. Much of this document, however, was lies or half truths designed simply to encourage the judge to take action against me. It is a known and documented fact that the Section 35 law can be abused. Folks who are angry at you, harbor resentments, or seeking revenge can twist truths and legally take away all your rights, and that's exactly what my "brother" did.

A section 35 can be a valuable tool when appropriately used and again, it saved my life, but I was already actively taking steps to do that myself, and that choice was taken from me. I can't help but to firmly believe that I was sectioned, in part, out of anger and revenge, using half-truths, some lies, and pure speculation. In recovery, we are constantly reminded to let go of toxic people in our lives, even if they are family. Make yourself number one. If you are sectioned, odds are that you needed help. I know I did and most people come to accept and forgive their petitioner, or so I'm told. Unfortunately, I am not ready for that, you might not be ready either; understandably so. Just be grateful to your higher power that you were saved, no matter how you got there, and ask for his grace in saying goodbye to your addiction and the toxic people who may have contributed to it.

SHACKLES

They shackled my feet
cuffed up my hands
threw me in a cell
then the back of a van
and the driver kept driving
as rough as he can
no seatbelts, he got pleasure
from hurting this man
as soon as we got there
they made me stand naked
they checked EVERY crevice
oh trust me they did.
They took my belongings
They took all my clothes
They x-ray'd my body
and poked ALL my holes
unless they've lived through it
nobody knows

they violated
this fragile man
desperately looking
for contraband

dignity, what?
dignity, what?
even my "back door"
was opened and shut.

SO, when you're sitting there asking
"Why's he so mad?"
Cause you took away every ounce of dignity I had.

ADDICTION IS THE REASON I FIND MYSELF HERE

I wake with a startle
and realize where I am
routine morning shock therapy
confused, disillusioned, simmer soaked regret
sore, head spinning bewilderment

INSTANT
"Oh my God, what did I do?"
INSTANT
"How'd I get here?" and "Fuck, I miss you"
INSTANT
"Damn it!" and "How do I get back?"
INSTANT
realization, I've run off the tracks
INSTANT
awareness of the rough patch ahead
INSTANT
humility, because I'm not dead
INSTANT
remorse for the things that I've done
INSTANT
fear cause I don't remember some!

And then reality hits me
addiction is the reason I find myself here
I miss you but it's over, that's pretty clear
and damn it, fuck this, I don't wanna go back
I wanna stay sober and get back on track!
Awareness, humility, remorse and fear;
addiction is the reason I find myself here

So, though I am broken, things could be worse.
I could have a procession following my hearse
but I have the chance to repair all this hurt
to be sober instead of six feet under dirt
I'll stay the course and do all the work
I'll embrace staying clean for all that it's worth
but when I wake in a startle, I must be sincere…
ADDICTION IS THE REASON I FIND MYSELF HERE

DETOX

SweAtY

NaUTiOuS

TopSY TurVY

ShAKy

voMItING

rEsTLEss

FEElInG LIkE SHIT

IrrITABle

AnGrY

SeiZuRES

They're watching me closely
as I toss in this bed
and every few hours
they give me some meds
this is the feeling
I constantly dread
my body in chaos
lost in my head
withdrawal, a nightmare
I'd rather be dead
these feelings make me
want to use instead
Please God let this pass,

ANGER MANAGEMENT

What are your triggers?
What makes you mad?
Know what provokes and instigates you.
Know how you react to negativity and threats.
Identify what upsets you and how you react to it.
Then stop. Breathe.
Try to control yourself and think before taking action.
Sometimes we bottle shit up.
Then explode at the tiniest thing.
Sometimes we act out or take our anger and frustration out on the wrong people.
We can destroy relationships and lives, including our own.
Stop. Breathe.
Try to conceive
just how much better
that your life can be
if you handle your anger
a bit differently.
It doesn't mean that you don't have the right to be angry.
Anger is a perfectly normal human emotion
but it can be destructive to you and those around you when handled poorly.
It can have physical and emotional repercussions.
So stop. Breathe
Handle it differently.

HERE I SIT IN RECOVERY GROUP

Here I sit in recovery group
being asked to color and paint.
It's happened more times
than I can count,
a "recovery group" this aint!
Now, one could argue art therapy
is about learning to heal
but it happens so much
I'm at the end of my rope
these filler classes are unreal!
I want to sit inside a group
and learn and listen and share,
discuss addiction amongst ourselves
not braid each other's hair.
This might sound controversial
I know that art has it's worth.
Creativity always has value
but more academia wouldn't hurt!

LET IT OUT

SCREAM if you want to
just find a safe place to do it.
If you're mad and wanna punch someone
Hit the bag or the gym just screw it!
If you feel the need to cry or weep
just find a box of tissues
and if you feel the need to be heard
give no one the chance to dismiss you.
Jump!
Wave your arms!
Dance for the happy, when you feel it
if you happen to have some kind of feeling
don't be afraid to reveal it….

Let It Out

JAILS, INSTITUTIONS AND DEATH

I got lucky
I found myself in an institution
Not dead or locked up
maybe YOU won't be so lucky

They say addicts end up in "jails, institutions or dead"
I was close to jail or worse....death
so close that I actually subconsciously prepared for it
nearly accepted it as an inevitability
rapidly approaching
but I got lucky
maybe YOU won't be so lucky.

Maybe you've been sectioned,
maybe you're locked in a cell,
but you're alive!

Addiction is forever
but sobriety can last just as long
it takes work
and it's not easy.

I got lucky
I'm not dead or locked up
but if we remain sober
we won't need luck!

HIGHER POWER

Depending on the path you choose, recovering from addiction quite often incorporates the need for you to recognize a higher power, something greater than yourself. While on your healing journey you might notice everyone keeps saying the "Our Father" and citing "Jesus", don't let that discourage you if you aren't a religious person. Everyone's higher power is different. Yes, for some people, a God is their higher power. For others, like myself, something like nature, or the earth or sun or moon is their higher power. Choose something that brings you peace and serenity, motivation and guidance; choose an entity that you feel is much bigger than yourself! Make that your focal point, your deity and your hope.

I'LL DO THE REST

Preacher, Preacher
pray for me; sing
pray for me; sing
pray for me; sing

Preach the good word
that I might do the right thing
do the right thing
do the right thing

Pastor, Pastor
bless and anoint
bless and anoint
bless and anoint

CAUSE I'M CRAVING SOME NIPS AND A LINE AND A JOINT

So dear preacher, dear pastor
please sing, preach and bless,
God grant me the serenity
and I'll do the rest.

CUFFS

The feeling of force
as they draw back your arms
the cold steel
click, click, clicks
tighter and tighter
around your wrists
they guide your head down
as they place you in the cruiser
back passenger's seat
cold leather
scrunching under you
as you uncomfortably try
to reposition.
Immobility, restraint,
the static, grumbled sound
from the CB radio
blue lights flash red
red lights flash blue
equipment, barriers, questions, mug shots
fingerprints,
waiting
waiting
WAITING
bail
begging
court
punishment.
TIME TO GET BETTER

LEMONADE

My drunken self is like
a car that's a lemon
the windshield is so foggy
I can't see
and everything in the rear view mirrors
are blurrier than they seem.
Step on the gas
and it comes to a stop,
step on the brake
and screw up the clock
the engine fills up
with dust, soot and smoke
so open the windows
or you're libel to choke.
Oh wait, you can't
the windows are broke.
So much to fix,
the mistakes that I've made
but I'll turn this lemon
into lemonade!

PAPER PLANES

Do you remember making paper planes? To make the tip of the plane you would take a piece of paper, fold the sides together until the edges met in a triangle. Then, with a few more simple folds you would have wings and maybe even a fancy tail.

Personally, I always had trouble matching my folds just right and meeting the ends perfectly. They would be uneven or wonky prompting the plane to fly improperly and take a nosedive right into the ground. Sometimes my paper planes would soar through the air, other times it was a crash and burn situation.

Dear fellow addict, life is like making paper planes. Sometimes you're going to have trouble making ends meet but you also have the opportunity to soar.

RISE UP

Elevate yourself

      Ascend

          Rise up!

People are going to make assumptions about you. You are going to know judgement, isolation and stigma. It will compound your existing trauma, triggers and pain. It will double your tears and diminish your spirit. It will take you down, it will drag you down. SO:

Elevate yourself

      Ascend

          Rise up!

REBORN

I want to accomplish so much
and influence this world courageously
but I dug myself an Olympic sized hole
and jumped recklessly
head first,
into the deep end,
and if that weren't bad enough
I dragged everyone down with me
and put others at risk
I feel so overwhelmed
dependent and scared
I feel so all alone
alone and unclothed
curled
in the fetal position
….waiting to be reborn

CINDERELLA'S BALL

Cinderella's Ball
Cinderella's Ball
Chandeliers
ballgowns that blossom and twirl
embroidered in gold
press up against tuxes
they glide, glide, glide…..waltz
and the wait staff come round
with flutes of champagne
effervescing a bubbly, golden tune
that of a siren
a calling
a summons
sequestering me
an invitation delivered
past the best of me
right to the part I detest in me
the part that's slowly
digesting me
FUCK, is this really my destiny?
spin spin twirl….
a 12 step dance.

FOCUS

I don't mean to be indelicate
but what the actual fuck?
They put me under a microscope
and cranked the power up
they turned the focus left to right
until they saw what they wanted to see
stigmatized and monochromatic
they saw only the monster in me

Did they forget all the good I've done?
Did they forget my charity?
Did they forget what I've done for THEM?
Did they forget about me?

Am I
Nothing
A burden
Insignificant
A no one
OR
Are they
Just fed up
With the things
That I've Done?

They don't mean to be indelicate
but after all of the things that I did
I must earn their forgiveness now
and also learn to forgive.

DRIVE

I've spent so much time dwelling in the past that I rarely look forward at all.
I've spent so much time curled up and crying that I rarely stand up and stand tall.
I've spent so much time hanging around tigers, I'm used to being mauled by their claws
I press the rewind button so frequently I've forgotten to stop and press pause.

I drink at the bar
until I am a mess
go home with strangers
for anonymous sex
sniffing on poppers
skin, spit and sweat
I remember their names
until I forget.
My mind, it races
fireworks, explosions,
synapse overdrive
gray matter erosion
I can't juggle these balls
I can't even throw them
I stumble and slur
I'm not even joking.

It's time to switch gears
from reverse into drive
and if I stay clean
I just might survive.

I CHOOSE ME

I wanna live life
unencumbered
especially if
my days are numbered
I wanna find peace
and hopefully keep her
especially if
peace is my teacher
I want to live a life
that's emblazoned
sober, no longer
lost and dazed and…
confused
like the times that I used
the drugs and the booze
fucked my life up times two
it's now time to choose….

and I choose me.

FUCK IT

Fuck it
fuck this
it's all just
bullshit
fuck groups
fuck me
I'm tired of being
stuck on repeat
it's the same old topics
the same old forms
the awkward silence
the awkward norms
what I really need is to get out of this place
I can't even get a pillowcase
it takes actual weeks to get anything done
and my counselor's been missing since fucking day one.
The food is so bad, well I shouldn't spoil it
let's just say that it came from the toilet
officers sing love songs in the halls at 3A
get me the fucking fuck out of this place
no soap in the bathroom, piss on the seats
this place is a vacuum sucking life outta me
so fuck it
fuck this
it's all just
bullshit
Oh, and that 3am singer is gonna get hit!

VINDICTIVE PURJURY

Will they ever understand me,
understand that I'm still a good guy,
forgive all the shitty things I did
at least before I die
will they understand that
there are reasons why I cry
mechanisms behind the pain I feel
watering my eyes?

They say I should forget about the past
but have they never learned about scars?
I'm sorry I need to process my shit
I just regret doing it in bars
regret not confiding my pain to a shrink
regret telling my cousin and brother,
repeatedly in the last twenty years
they've hurt me one way or another....
both of them are users
of violence and misdirection
but when I finally did it myself
they planned a fucking section
I should have known!
I did know
but I was desperate and homeless
with nowhere to go.
BEHIND EVERY GLASS THEY SEE
THEIR LIVES ARE A CATASTROPHE
IT WAS EASIER TO MAKE AN ASS OF ME
PUT ME ON BLAST VINDICTIVELY
VINDICTIVELY
THEY SECTIONED MY ASS VINDICTIVELY
I READ THE PETITION OF PURJURY
NOW THERES NO WAY OF DETERRING ME
IM PREVENTING THEM FROM EVER HURTING ME
FURVIDLY
AGAIN
PERMENANTLY
BY SAYING GOODBYE.

STARS ARE ALWAYS BORN WITH AN EXPLOSION
BLOOD COMES FROM BONES AND
FIRE FROM STONES AND
DON'T BORROW ANYONE'S THRONE
CREATE YOUR OWN, FRIEND

DEATH, DARKNESS, DIET GINGER ALE

Sipping, I'm sipping
can you follow my trail
through Death, Darkness and Diet Ginger Ale?
The silence, the silence
the flavor, the fizz
though I keep sipping
I don't know what this is.
My record is skipping
I'm picking these scabs.
I guess that accounts
for the scars that I have.
The wounds I create
reopen and bleed
oblivion, oblivion
desire to succeed.
This snow capped mountain
The emperor's Queen
they think I'm confused
but I know what I mean
They gather their kindle, assemble the pyre.
They set up the stage; prop up the barbed wire.
They tie me up tightly and start up their fire.
They burn me up quickly and take my empire.

So I sit at the bar and sip on this drink
into the darkness I steadily sink
closer to death I follow the trail
into Death, Darkness, Diet Ginger Ale

IN THE HALLS OF THE HOUSE OF ILL REPUTE

The autumnal breeze gathers the leaves in clusters outside the front door.
I walk up the path, like Dickens or Plath, knowing fully of just what's in store.
And soon as I enter, I hear sounds of splendor enticing me in a bit more.
Temptation surrounds me, addiction has found me, I'm craving like never before.

I stand in the foyer a scandalous voyeur, eager to start to peruse
knowing full well that each hall I dwell has plenty of options to use.
The dim lit soft candles and fancy door handles tell me there's nothing to lose
inside each suite are various treats designed to alter one's mood.

The first room I pass features a glass of bourbon gold and compelling
and before I can think, I guzzle that drink and soon my senses start swelling.
A couple doors down, I notice a sound, not calling my name but yelling,
it's a glass of malbec that I drink in a sec, without even swishing or smelling.

Behind every door somethings in store, alluring, sequestering me
and deep down I know, I should turn and go, my conscience is pestering me.
There's morphine in vials somewhere down these aisles
cocaine spread in pretty white lines
and if I walk a bit more, behind one of these doors
is some Xanax to make me unwind.
Pretty pills
fentanyl
tourniquets
and meth
I'm becoming a ghost after every dose
slowly cascading regret.

I wish I never entered these halls, I wish I never messed with this shit.
I wish I never screwed up my life, I wish I never wasted my gifts.
I thought I could control my substance abuse but alas no one can refute.
I should have never entered these halls, in the house if ill repute.

WITH EASE THE STAINS OF DISTAIN AREN'T ERASED

"I'm sorry" if we're lucky enough to get it, isn't always sufficient to absolve.
Minds, though often intelligent, think around them Earth revolves.
Everyone's story has unique iteration in which they place true belief
but love's not a creature of consideration, it's a selfish and self-serving thief.
First it took my confidence, then it took my trust.
Gave false hope about the future, gave false hope about us.
Vows! Vows?
Tell me how
"in sickness and health"
is meaningless now.
Lies, Lies!
Not even goodbye.
I can't tell you I'm sorry
or that Moxy died.
There were so many ways for us to divide,
couldn't you choose one where I could've survived?
Out of every pain that I've ever felt
this is the worst hand I've ever been delt.

I wallow, I suffer, I toss, turn and sweat.
I'm filled with such torment, longing and regret.
I flounder, I stumble, I'm in so much pain.
Should I feel comfort, or embrace the disdain?
These tears stain my pillow as they pour down my face,
with ease these stains of disdain aren't erased.

JAWS OF LIFE

It hurts
I'm scared
it hurts
so bad
it hurts
and I can't
convey to anyone just how much pain I have.

Everyone knows the monster I was
but no one knows why or cares
they find it easier to dismiss me goodbye
and resume life as if I'm not there.

Pry me out
pry me out
claw me out of this mess.
Pry me out
pry me out
set me free.
The monster is gone; I've put him to rest
If I maintain sobriety.

SCRAMBLED EGGS

There's yolk in my teeth!
There's yolk in my teeth!
creamy yellow collections
smeared conveniently
like mayo on a burger
or guac, slimy green
tsetse flies buzz
and land right between
my teeth
my teeth
they dine and they feast
on the yolk in my teeth
on the yolk in my teeth!

My eggs are fucking scrambled
from walking on these shells
life is a disaster,
boiling water hell.
Christ on a cannoli
lemon in my eyes
sometimes I just wanna tell
all these assholes "BYE"

DEAR CHEF

I'm writing you this letter
in hopes your ways will change
you see, I'm diabetic
and your meal plan brings me pain.
The nurse checks my blood sugar
morning and afternoon
and every time, these numbers of mine
are frankly over the moon!

It's not because I'm cheating
on candy bars and cake
it's because there's so much sugar
in every meal you make.
Are you trying to kill me?
Poison me with carbs?
Are your main ingredients
syrup mixed with lard?

Take your "Sweedish meatballs"
and shove them up your ass.
I'd rather chew my toenails
out of boredom after class.

Take your "red sauce" pasta
and rotten celery stick
down to Market Basket
where you can suck a dick.

Speaking of dick sucking,
what's it gonna take
for me to get some protein?
All the meat is FAKE!

Hyperglycemic
Hyperglycemic
Guacamole and kraut
I need a bunch of insulin
because the nurse ran out!
All in all uncertainty, none in so much pain,
I never wanna eat another meal you made again!

DOMINOES TIP, CLICK AND FALL

Right out of the box I used alcohol
so innocuously
innocently
naively, I walked confidently
invincibly barefoot
through life
ignorantly assuming that I would never trip, fall or stub my toes
ignorantly assuming that I would never step on a rusty needle or nail
that the only blades in life were the soft comforting blades of grass that foraged and
slipped between my toes as I glided unscathed through the lawn as a child.

I got so used to socially drinking, then drinking for relief, then drinking habitually that
ultimately I sought alcohol for everything. It became my way to relieve stress, all stress.
But life progresses, stressors can intensify and with that progression my drinking
coincided…until:

The more intense the problem, the more intense the drinking
The more intense the consequences, the more confused thinking.
The road to life isn't always easy street, existing isn't always a blast,
bad shit happens to good people too, there are often snakes in the grass.
We have to work at our problems, not guzzle them out of a glass
there's also blades in lawnmowers that'll slice your fucking ass

So don't think you're invulnerable, use caution in your life.
Rough patches are inevitable, so are moments of strife.
Be prepared, resist temptation, love you, cope well and stand tall.
It's easy to succumb to the cravings, but then dominoes tip, click, fall.

DIGGING

Digging and digging,
got me a shovel
my substance abuse
has got me in trouble
and if I keep going
I get mean and shout
go a bit further
I lash and black out

Digging and digging
I've started to dig
my small drinking problem
is suddenly big
at first when I'd drink
I'd stumble and slur
but as I continue
my vision gets worse
go a bit further
soon I'm a wreck
maybe fall dancing
or have risky sex

Digging and digging
each time I'm hurt
I dig a bit more
I bring up more dirt
no longer a dancer
no longer a flirt
just a prolific asshole
disrespectful and curt

Bartender, get me a double, I'm digging and digging and booze is my shovel,
substance abuse keeps bringing me trouble, get me into rehab and out of this bubble.

FADES AWAY

It all fades away
everything fades
it all disappears
it all fades away
immunosuppressing
leaves us all weak
a superinfection
invades as we speak
it gets in your bloodstream
it glides like a worm
leaving you ravaged
transparent, infirm
infantile
infantile
ageing in reverse
everything fades away
but using makes it worse.

THE GREAT CEREBRAL INVASION

A soft yet festering plague has invaded, taken up root
and has begun the complicated process of unwinding, it sorta tickles.
Has it ever occurred to you that your incessant self-righteous and inaccurate
assessments have led to serious delusional conclusions?
Consequences have consequences.
Straighten up, stand, act right-
Purr if it makes you feel pretty
and if pretty makes you feel liked.
And the soldier cells hunker down
camouflaged and blended between mitochondrial sacs and a rogue synapse.
Have you ever found yourself encased here?
The view is quite disorderly but captures the eye.

You created an entire dossier if deceitful inaccuracies, devious twists of the lemon
and presented it to a judge.
Perjured yourself.
I never entered rehab, therefore never checked myself out
there was no bases for a section when I was voluntarily going.
And in the court hall I asked you to let me have the chance to do it myself
but you took that choice away from me
you took my liberty away from me
you took my freedom away from me
Tell me, would it have been different if you and I weren't actively mad at each other
fighting for the billionth time?
You mean to say that your petition of embellishments and actual lies wasn't born out of
revenge?

Recovery teaches us to forgive but it also reinforces how necessary it is to distance
oneself from toxic, harmful relationships or end them altogether. Give me housing, then
pull the rug. Promise a phone then pull the plug. I should have known. You're incapable
of love. Enough is enough. No medical knowledge but try to diagnose me, when I tell
you I'm sick you don't believe!? I forgive you, please forgive me.
Goodbye.

COME TO MY JAIL CELL

Come to my jail cell
I need a diversion
sex talk is fun
but I need it in person
outside of this place
I like it romantic
but you can just fuck me
under these circumstances
we don't need to kiss
or share an embrace
just pull down those shorts
and thrust in my face
throb with me
throb with me
get naked and sweaty
and bob with me
turn down the lights
be a slob with me
share your humungous
knob with me
there really is
no stopping me
come to my jail cell
just check in the halls
so the CO's won't see
me empty your balls
come to my jail cell
this hunger won't cease
we might be in prison
but I'll grant you release!

SHADOWS OF SHARP TEETH BEVELS AND LUMENS

The hallways are empty in the methadone clinic
but not in the locked up psych ward
they gathered up those with dual diagnoses
and enforced the "Addicts Accord"
We the people are unrecognized
when suffering this pervasive disease
the level, the level of their sterile bevel
transference brings such disbelief.

Clowns
Clowns
Clowning around
all over the locked ward
in hospital gowns
drinking the Kool-Aid
in mounds and mounds
in order to get the sedatives down.
Some of them grinning
a methodical grin
some of them scratching
at dry flaky skin
some of them frantic
trying to escape
out of their locked chairs
and tightened restraints
some eyes are vacant
with mouths dripping drool
others are crying
the tears of a fool
and the visitors question.....they question and question
our "sordid behavior"... our pallored complexion
nothing they see in their own self reflection
will send them spinning in the right direction.
Shadows of sharp teeth dance on the ceiling
injectable drugs pierce without feeling
with a bevel so sharp it glides in the lumen
I MIGHT BE AN ADDICT BUT IM ALSO A HUMAN

THE WILDLY UNSCRUPULOUS BLATHER IN MY UNEASY MIND

Suit up gentlemen, double zip, double zip
you don't want my Covid, I don't want your shit
giddy up, giddy up, prickle with spurs
Romeo gunfire, vexatious slurs
assuredly your impurity
does not reassure
that you'll be compliant
refined and demure
Thanksgiving, Christmas, New Years alone
had the cops escort me out of my home
Mom, Dad, and Moxy are dead now, they're gone
my husband forgot I exist and moved on
so strip down gentlemen, stop, take a bow
scrub up to your neckline, scrub up and scrub down
I lit the bomb's fuse but it doused before blowing
I'm like a cat ninja all stealth like tip toeing
I took a few cheap shots at my marriage a fizzle
unfairly he fired back with a nuclear missel
sadistic
sadistic
let's be realistic
marriage has a point
and clearly he missed it
he did terrible things but I got him assistance
but when I needed help
he left and dismissed it
and everything we had.

TAKEN AWAY
(With Love Like Yours)

I was homeless and you offered me a home
but you took it away, you took it away
So I was a foolish to accept
your offer for a phone
cause you took that away, you took that away
even when you promised we'd spend time alone
you took it away, you took it away.
You never acknowledge the fault in your actions
gaslighting me with your senseless retractions
time spent with you always ends in disaster
hate and revenge are all that you're after
Admit it, it wasn't some show of love
when you perjured yourself in front of that judge
you had been harboring a furious grudge
you needed a reason and I gave you that nudge
took my freedom from me like the rest of that stuff.
Greg took my marriage but you killed my soul
left me with nothing and nowhere to go
all that meant something you took back or stole
if destructions your mission then you've met your goal

I'm happy alone now
love myself everyday
and not even YOU
can TAKE THAT away!

YOU ARE AN ADDICT

You are an addict
and everyone knows it
let the assumptions and stigma begin
moreover, be attentive
because they are also going to make you their scapegoat
because you're vulnerable, and they can,
and they will.

FROM NOW ON:
if you utter one lie, you're always the liar
light just one match, now you set every fire
if something goes missing you're automatically the thief
and they won't hesitate to call the police
and who do you think the police will believe
You are an addict
and that's all they will see

And you'll want to scream and cry when you know that you're right
but no one believes you and it's not worth the fight
it's a silent blustery cross to bear
No longer innocent until proven guilty
but….

You are an addict
you're strong and resilient
prove them all wrong
show them your brilliant
let no one demean you
or give you hell
the best revenge
is living well.

THE DERBY

We seem to be at a
juxtaposition
my life's not a derby
for your demolition
though you're my blood
you're no accrementition
our ties have long suffered
severe malnutrition
until the point
of decomposition

and it rots and it rots
you can smell it, it rots
it's foul and I'm not
gonna take your cheap shots
no more

I'm off of my knees now
they're bruised and they're sore
but I give you release now
you won't see me
no more

I bet you feel
satisfaction galore
got your revenge inside of that court
threw out the keys after locking the door
this isn't resentment, it's not even war
I deserve better treatment, I deserve more

LET ME IN
(It's okay to lean on others for support)

I'll catch you when you lose your balance and slip
I'll love you, your flaws, and companionship
it's not easy but I'll hold your hand through this shit
let me in
let me in
I was there

I know it's not easy when your entire world alters
I know it's a challenge when you lose ground and falter
your mother misses your sweet face so call her
let me in
let me in
I was there

life's messy waters absorb like a sponge
tree trunks grow roots thanks to the sun
it rises
I know
I was there

I guess what I'm saying is that you're not alone
there's people around you, you have a smart phone
you're always welcome and loved in my home
so let me in
let me in
I am here

IN THE GARDEN OF ROSES AND HYMNS

There in the garden of roses and hymns

everything's magic and blows with the wind

There's butterfly nests mixed in the vines

Icicles form even in summertime

Birds dance with squirrels and kiss honeybees

And marshmallow s'mores grow from the trees

There in the garden of roses and hymns

There's elves in bright colors with little cleft chins

There's fairies and otters and creatures with wings

There's owl that who and lilacs that sing

It rains glitter drops that reflect off the sun

And the golden sunlight warms up everyone

There's never a tear unless when reminiscing

No struggles or fears just passionate kissing

Every nerve ending of your body just twitches

And there's a well of intentions for only well wishes

It's always dusk but the sun never sets

no heart ache, disappointment, pain, or regrets

There's bushes of skittles and shrubs that grow pizza

And half naked Romans with fig leafs to greet ya

It smells just like sugar there's ribbons and flavor

Moments to cherish, seconds to savor

Life only ends when you don't let it begin

There in the garden of roses and hymns

FACING MYSELF

(Find healthy ways to cope with loss, avoid drugs and alcohol, they will make it worse)

I'm not really sure what made me self destruct

Maybe just maybe the wrong wire was cut

Spun like a top then out of control

Taking me over and taking it's toll

Hurt everybody that I loved the most

A parasite sucking the life from my host

Over and over I asked you to leave

But it was only because I didn't want u to see

What kind of monster I'd turned out to be

But it was too late I lost u for life

yes it's too late I lost you for life.

Still I'm glad that your well I'm glad your alright

I'm glad that your happy and smiling tonight

And I hope you get all u ever dreamed of

a home, and a family, and most of all love

My monster is gone now and I'm standing tall

you leaving my life was my wake up call

and for a short time we shared the same road

my love will not die or ever grow old

Sorry for lying and making you cry

Doing bad things and saying goodbye

ran from u cause you saw thru my disguise

And for that my love I apologize

But it's too late I lost you for life

yes, it's too late I lost you for life

POETRY
(Art is a healthy way of coping and expressing your emotions)

it's in you

when all those little moments

that seemed insignificant

get significance, have a meaning

and you understand the bigger picture

the worlds symmetry

making you feel

something more

something incredible

something moving

something

a spark

that makes you recall

Revisit

You just know

you're part of a

picture much bigger than you.

JUST ONE LIGHT

All we need sometimes is just one light
just one person saying it'll be all right
just one voice offering hope
and when you want to give up
they strictly say no
and it's usually the person you'd never expect
what we want in this world ain't always what we get
they lift your head up off the pillow
they lift up your spirits when you're feeling them willow
they don't walk away they don't just dismiss you
no, they are the ones offering a tissue
Just one light, just one voice,
reminding you gently,
that there's always a choice,
offering just one listening ear,
hearing the things you don't want them to hear
letting you know they still love you when you just might not love yourself anymore...

All I just needed was to hear your story,
you offered me hope, God offered his glory...
with faith and hope and through our lord's name
just one bright light can become a flame.

ACCEPTANCE

DENY that it's happened, (this can't be real?)

it must be a dream, I'm numb, I can't feel.

I'm pissed that you left me, I'm ANGRY as hell.

I been crying so long that my eyes start to swell.

Still I asked God to make this a really bad dream

I'll be a better person, I start BARGAINING

I'm avoid any feeling until reality sets in

then stricken with sadness, I feel DEPRESSION

Feel it, feel it, allow time to cry

Scream out I love you

Scream out goodbye

Ask for forgiveness

Beg God for more time

I did all these things

for one friend of mine….

And then I found peace…

ACCEPTANCE

KEEP WONDERING

where do we go

when they tell us there's no more road left

but everyone around us

can breathe, and move, can live?

do we fight for our lives?

do we pray?

do we see what others can't

until they get to the end themselves?

they can give orders

opinions

prescribe

but they never truly feel

what you're feeling

inside

the rest of the world

is up and bathing

as we gasp for breath

we're suffocating

begging for comfort

begging for sleep

begging for something

tasty to eat

asking for healing

asking for peace

I honestly still wonder

what all of this means

I won't stop advocating for you.

LOVE DOES NOT STOP

True love

Real love

Comes by rarely

And when u find it

Hold on to it tightly

Never let go

Fight for it

Make compromises

Communicate

Always say I love u

Before going to bed

Wake up in the morning

And look at him

And know

How special you have it....

Love

Hold on to it tightly

Fight for it

And cherish it

Forever

LOVE DOES NOT STOP

THE INCREDIBLE THINGS

sometimes get caught up in the dilemmas of life

family, health, aging work, and it's strife

there's pain, it can hurt and it cuts like a knife

but there's ways to survive and sleep well every night

you gotta do something to take care of your self

go to beach, listen to shells

enjoy family night even though it can be drama

get on the phone and talk to your mama

talk to your lover and look in his eyes

try to hold hands or cuddle at night

carve a big pumpkin and then make it glow

take a hot bath and sink deep below

look at the sky and examine the clouds

cry when your hurt or scream really loud

bake yourself cookies say a little prayer

for your higher power will always be there

the bad, the good, the edible things

a candle, and the joy that the smell of it brings

you and the ocean and the shell as it sings

my family although they meddle in things

the look in your eyes is one hell of a thing

Deep in the Dimension of Halos and Wings

never give up or settle with things

one day at a time and it's better it seems

they're simple, they're subtle

they're the incredible things

FLOWERS

We live in a completely uncertain world- everything is fluid- one moment it is ours and the next it is some distant memory that we look back upon (with a teardrop and a smile if we are lucky). From the moment we are conceived there is this constant struggle/tugging of variables that somehow can either destroy us or keep us thriving..... in the womb one chemical exchange in either direction can possibly make the difference between someone developmentally delayed and someone who successfully walks the city streets with a suitcase and more than occasional dirty secret (one or the other may be just as bad).

And then we might get the chance to grow, and fall both before and after we learn to walk. Bittersweetly we might get the chance to kiss adolescence and taste its glittery love heartbeat golden sun filled rainstorm- two parents or one- we learn what we were meant to understand of the sky and the soil and everything between that moves and swims and sweats and curls all fetal like when it is in real pain.

And so somewhere in that tangled mess we learn that those flowers we smelled when we were younger and more appreciative are so much lower than eye-level and that there is so much to distract our eyes as we get taller and older- eventually it's really easy to miss them..

And we meet people, eyes that enchant, words that repel, and ears that allow so much to come in yet acknowledge a fraction.... and we try to perfect that sitcom comedy drama fairy tale, horror, still reminiscent from our younger and more hopeful reveries, we are left with thoughts of forever love turned to October leaves- we have successes measured by individual standards and we have failures that others might experience as a success....

Consider that at any given time everything can change and everything can petrify.... and in times like these, messy and complicated we find ourselves twittered and tantured and boiling- brewing- fucking, or making new life- weather or not conception occurs- I feel empowered and afraid simultaneously when I am with you- and I don't want to be a prefix or suffix....

I want to be another syllable. Still history, and society, and life and every odd- and every predictor- hell even everyone seems to foreshadow that we will end- but what the fuck ever really goes on forever? Only very few things...that I am too young and green and distorted by pride to understand...... there are the few things that last forever..... and so then why worry about forever if forever, by definition, will never really fade.... my only desire is that I can hold on tight to the special parts of this show, like you, for as long as I can before the odds and stars and destiny all stack up together and weigh up against us, and the credits roll messily.... I just want to enjoy our time together- looking up toward the great times, looking all around at what the world has to offer us as individuals and possibly a team, and most appreciatively looking down- enjoying the flowers. so even though now I am older I might walk with my head down but on occasion it's just because I am trying to still appreciate the flowers

CHARITY, OH CHARITY

Charity, oh charity, why can't you see he's not right
you call me each night at three in the morning in fear of your beautiful life
there's 911, and safe houses, there's hotlines, and groups for support,
I know the black and blue marks on your skin aren't cause you tripped on the floor

Charity, oh Charity, the world's full of shit, and contempt
there's so much corruption, disease, and distortion, it leaves us a little verklempt
I know that you love him, you'll do anything, to stop the violent abuse
but he feeds on your vulnerabilities, until you've lost all you can lose.

When you walked through the door inside my apartment wearing your Louis V. shades
I knew there was a bruise behind ur sunglasses, I knew there were bruises in spades
he's brought you to the brink of death, yet your persistence keeps you by his side
but there's bruises, and welts, and discolored abrasions that even sunglasses can hide

I got to my door and took off my shoes, I'm crying and wearing all black
I wish somehow, that I could have done something, I wish we could take it all back.
you're funeral services, and all who attended, seemed like a nasty nightmare
none of this shit could have ever happened, if I tried harder to be present and there

He hit you and beat you, you cried, sweat and bled,
all of your loved ones and all your best friends
knew that he'd leave you, or leave you for dead
why'd you ignore us, you watched us all beg

a note, then a chorus, a bridge and refrain
a song that we sing while lamenting in pain
he destroyed you're youth, you had only a glimpse
he took your existence and your innocence

Equality, bulimia, what about transgendered rights,
nuclear arms, marathon bombs and planes that disappear overnight
teens on a cruise ship that's now under water,
the worlds filled with chaos, heartbreak and disorder
a woman gunned down by her Olympic amputee,
a mom who drove her kids to the sea,
kids in the gutter with nothing to eat

Charity, Oh Charity

MOMENTS OUTLANDISH LAVISH AND SUCH

While at the local supermarket a tall man made his way to me. When he got close, I realized that he worked there but there was something more. This man, seven feet tall, missing most of his teeth looked like the hunchback of Notre Dame. I'm not trying to be sarcastic or rude here, this is what he looked like. He was clearly mentally delayed, he could not speak, he'd only grunt as he would point to objects with a smile or facial expression that depicted his emotion. After he began pointing to several objects in my basket I explained to him that I was making dinner tonight. He pointed to my hair, and I couldn't help but giggle, and get misty eyed.

As I cashed out I congratulated the manager on having the disabled community take such a presence in the store. But then after driving home I realized that there was something more to our interaction, perhaps a gift of sorts; a revelation. This man, who very clearly lives at a disadvantage, who faces difficulty with daily living, and a life filled with obstacles, couldn't have a bigger and more innocent smile. He was not fake smiling to welcome a customer, he was genuinely happy. He simply wanted to interact with another human being, and enjoy the day.

I highly doubt that this man will ever own a mansion, or have a wild car, or CEO position- but he smiled like he did. I think that this brief interaction was one that I really needed lately. I can get so caught up in wanting to have the best stuff, designer jeans, elaborate dinners, wild adventures. And while it is way more important for me to change the world while I am here, I think that I appreciate life just a little bit more than I did before this interaction.

The moments outlandish lavish and such mean nothing without love interaction and touch, what's cosmic is not possessing so much but our ability to help others through compassion and love. Sometimes it's easier to see your troubles and fears you get caught up in cycles that fester for years but take a step back- there could be many more tears- appreciate, treasure, and relish in life- revere it, revere it, revere.....

The moments outlandish lavish and such- are always the meaningful moments I share with someone, and perhaps this was the best one of all lately!

GRATEFUL

Life has given us so much

good and bad

cooked and raw

fast forward and rewind

gravestones and roses

and little containers

to put our memories in

over and over

take them grab them and hold them tight

and keep your reflectors on in the dark

HAPPY WITH ME

Standing here

hoping it's good enough to be

what you've always wanted

behind the fact that I feel

like I don't belong anywhere

I don't have a space

to be only me

to stop and just breathe

one breath

so regularly

so free and at ease

with no one to please

but me

TORNADO MIKEY

There's wind in the air and storm clouds are forming

on the forecast today was a tornado warning

little did I know that tornado was me

I'm kicking up dust and knocking down trees

I'm spinning and spinning, with each turn I'm stronger

Not tied up, or lied to or weak any longer

defining myself more every day

and I'm taking what stands in my way

I'll rip out your home right at the foundation

confess to your maker cause you're 'bout to face him

All of the ropes and the chains and the twine

still weren't a match for these forces of mine

I'm driven by anger moved by revenge

fueled by the notion that we'll never be friends

So I stand in the center, and chant my commands

summons the wind with both of my hands

and the bright skies darken, black clouds gather in

they twist and they form and they move and they spin

I give them direction and power from the gods

I take a deep breath and give a slight nod

If anyone hurts you, seriously go fuck him

or break out your rock star of massive destruction

use all your powers to spin strong and live well

God doesn't sleep and it's real hot in hell!

HALF OF HALF

laid there crying

and you just sat back

coiled in the disclaimer

that I'm half of half

I laid there crying

and you actually laughed

dangling that carrot

the next scene in your act

I laid there crying

feeling guilt from the past

trying so hard

to get everything back

I laid there crying

like a fool, like an ass

and you just pretended

wearing that mask.

Crawling and stumbling and learning to walk again

I didn't realize how hard I was on myself

consumed with guilt

tortuous hell

and so now, I somehow, have learnt to catch my breath

I can't go back and change it all, but this isn't life or death!

I've learned to be a better man- grow strong, to smile, to laugh,

I deserve to be loved one hundo percent, not only half of half.

GOD'S PLAN

God didn't send you to me for love,
He sent you to teach me a lesson
He sent you to remind me what true love isn't
So when I find it I'll know it's a blessing
God didn't send you to me for support
Cause when I needed help you just bailed
He sent you to me to blow up my secrets
And leave my world fucked and derailed
God didn't send you to me for a partner
He sent you to me for a chapter
The story of us and our villainous ways remind me what I'm really after
God didn't send you to my life
Because he saw a potential
He sent you to me so that I would learn
That everything is consequential
He gave me the devil so one day I'd know
Without doubt the angel I found
He gave me our chapter so I'd understand
How low I fell foolishly to the ground
I guess in a nutshell our time was a gift
It paved roads for a future that's mature
I now know my weaknesses I now know my faults-
And I sure as hell have seen all of yours
I'll love you forever in some twisted way
And our time I will never forget
But you lost my heartbeat and impression of you
mostly you lost my respect
God didn't send you to me for forever
But your damage will last just as long
The blessing I get out of all this however
Is that life's better now that you're gone

UNDEAD

Somewhere last year old Michael died, the one that was sad the one that would cry

somewhere last year my heart stopped its beat, an evil someone sucked life out of me

somewhere the monster that I had become was trumped by vile and evil someone

he took every drop of the blood in my system, he took everything when without or when with him

and as I lay cold he would dance and he'd sing, like nothing was wrong, carefree little thing

but then I woke up, confused at the start, everything spinning, an unbeating heart

I drew all new breath inside of my lungs without knowing what I had become

sure he killed me, and stripped me of my life, but what resulted from that is a fucking surprise

my blood rid of toxins, my intentions grew clear, I may have died once cause of one silly queer

but never again, I was stronger, intense and something was different about every sense

my hearing was better, my speed had improved, my eyes hypnotized, men liked how I move

my cravings are different, and now I want blood and you're gonna pay for what you have done

you saw me crying, on the brink of death yet you ran and hid, you just tried to forget.

Transition was hard, the sun hurt my eyes, in bed's where I stayed, until the moonrise

I preferred the dark cause no one would see, just what kind of monster you made out of me

and then suddenly was a pain in my mouth, I felt it, it hurt, my fangs coming out

and when they had grown my thirst got severe, hunger for vengeance, profound loss of fear

and when it was over I fed and grew strong, realized that you were the monster all along

you took things from me that I'd never expect, sobriety, everything, you left me a mess

and I'm sure it was all part of your revenge, you'd cover with "love you" introduce me to friends

it took me so long to arrive where I am and I'll never again settle for just any man

I will never let someone strip me of my life my rebirth's been awesome, I know you weren't right

in the meantime I'm growing, I'm stronger, I feed, I'm better than ever, I'm better indeed

you'll never take another sad tear from me, my fangs are exposed and I love the new me.

TO THOSE WHO CHOOSE THE CHEMICAL WAY

To those who choose the chemical way everything always comes back
just because it's all fine today doesn't mean you won't fall off track
I know I know, it's easy and fun it's taboo, it's great and it's nice
but the truth of the matter is a matter of fact- It always affects people's lives
I sit here one hundred percent yet completely broken in two
I didn't think this would happen to me, don't let it happen to you
take the advice of someone who fell after always being on top
it takes control and scoops you right up till the point where you just cannot stop
we always talk of merriment times, times of fun and sheer joy
but the people you choose to hang around with can influence you in ways that destroy
it took me forever to get to this place but now I won't shut my mouth
not till I get my whole point across until you know what I'm talking about
it's easy to reach for the drugs or the booze, they're a quick fix for mind and the body
whenever you're sad or out at the club or hanging at someone's house party
but be strong and say no- they'll respect you for that, even if it is just you
it's better right now to open your mouth than to go through all I went through
I'm almost on top-I'm finding my way but damn this shit is intense
I'm young and I'm fun and I'm chemical free and got rid of all druggie friends
it's time for you to grab onto life and make sure it doesn't explode
say no to the drugs, and don't drink too much don't ever get out of control
trust me, believe me, cause I was once there medicating to drown out the tears
but the pain that results from any poor coping is a million times harder, and lasts years
Love Michael

SIR IN THE MIRROR

Sir, in the mirror, I'm glad you smile back, I didn't think I'd see you anymore

I was sad when you left, I played you guitar, wrote you poetry

but you just kept getting sadder, you stayed in bed all day

and cried....

Sir in the mirror, remember this view, remember this smile, in all that you do

let no one break you, protect your sweet heart

keep it together don't fall apart

remember your better than teardrops and beer

without all those bad times you'd never get here!!!!!

Sir, in the mirror, I love you so much,

and now that I know that I'll never give up

I'll never surrender, I'll never lose hope,

I'll avoid the unhealthy whenever I cope.

Sir, your reflection is warm like the sun

let no one take that

and I mean NO ONE!

YOU ARE A RAINBOW

his one is for Tyler Clementi, Asher Brown, Seth Walsh, Billy Lucas, and Justin Aaberg

It's for me when I was 18, for you when you were 17. It's for all of us.

You are not the only one scared inside yourself

you are not the only one living this pure hell

you are not the only one asking God for help

you are not the only one who's thought of killing yourself

but you gotta stand tall you gotta break free

there's people out there just like you there's people just like me

there's others out there willing to help in every community

the bullies, that make you insecure, they taunt and laugh, call names

they pride themselves in hurting you, the whole damn things a shame

but there's so much life out there to live, there's so much left to see

don't take your life, and all your gifts, in time I know you'll see

and all those bullies who teased me so are now long gone or dead

they're fat, in jail, or too coked out to understand what I just said

they lack success, they lack a brain on welfare; doing time

but I'm 40 and I'm fabulous and I haven't reached my prime!

I look the way I want to look wear glitter and tight jeans

I dance the local night club dry I'm sexy, I'm a dream

So when you feel you're in despair breathe deep; boy, this will pass

in time you're gonna grow; you'll see and you'll kick some ignorant ass

there's nothing like a homophobe blinded by their hate

to make you feel inadequate but they're time'll come; just wait!

So get out there and stand your ground be proud of who you are

fight hard, be strong, let's change this world you know that you're a star

don't let them get the best of you don't let them steal your shine

wear glitter, and make up, and love who you want

well beat this, one day at a time!

www.ingramcontent.com/pod-product-compliance
Lightning Source LLC
Chambersburg PA
CBHW080915260726
48661CB00009B/3672